Enlarging
Union in M...
and Eastern Eu~~~

Nicholas Hopkinson

January 1994

Wilton Park Paper 81

Report based on Wilton Park Conference WPS 93/7: 16–19
September 1993. Enlarging the European Community: The Impact
of EC Policies on New Members and Neighbouring States, in
association with the Finnish Ministry of Foreign Affairs at
Säätytalo, Helsinki

London: HMSO

ISBN 0 11 701799 X
ISSN 0953–8542

Contents

1 Introduction

Following the dissolution of the former Soviet Union (FSU), Finland and other neutral countries in Europe have felt much less constrained in their relations with the European Community, now the European Union (EU). The EU is still a pole of attraction, as indicated by the continuing wish of countries to apply for membership. This paper examines prospects for EU membership of the four current candidates, in particular Finland, and potential future candidates in the East.

The four European Free Trade Area (EFTA) applicants are all established democracies with developed welfare states and higher GNPs per capita than the average of current EU member states. The Lisbon Summit in 1992 decided that the EFTA countries can become members on condition that they adhere to the Maastricht Treaty and that the Delors II financial package is approved. After the agreement on the Delors package at the European Council in Edinburgh in December 1992, and taking into consideration the prospect of an early ratification of the Maastricht Treaty, the Council started accession negotiations with Austria, Finland and Sweden on 1 February 1993. After the Norwegian application for membership and the positive decision by the Council of Ministers, negotiations with Norway began on 5 April 1993. Applicants will be admitted provided that they fully accept the *acquis communautaire* (the arrangements previously agreed between existing member states) without prejudice to possible transitional measures decided during the negotiations.

In late 1992, the Council of Ministers approved the principal elements of the general negotiation framework, the procedure for negotiation and the structure of the negotiations. Twenty-nine chapters were listed under general headings: chapters almost fully covered by the European Economic Area (EEA) agreement between the EU and five of the seven EFTA countries (free movement of goods, freedom to provide services and the right of establishment, freedom of movement for workers, free movement of capital, transport policy, competition policy, consumer and health protection, research and information technologies, education, statistics and company law); chapters only partly covered by the EEA (social policy, environment, energy, agriculture, and fisheries); chapters in areas covered by the EU but not covered by the EEA (customs union, external relations, structural instruments, regional policy, industrial policy, taxation); areas introduced by the Maastricht Treaty (Economic and Monetary Union (EMU), Common Foreign and Security Policy (CFSP), and Justice and Home Affairs); and general chapters such as finance and budgetary provisions and institutional arrangements.

As EEA signatories, the four candidates have already accepted some 60 per cent of the content of the eventual accession treaties. Work between the Commission and candidate countries is well under way on all chapters. Even in chapters that were not officially opened, pending full ratification of the Maastricht Treaty, a considerable amount of preparatory work was completed at the technical level. By mid-September 1993, between seven and 29 negotiating chapters have been declared closed, depending on the country concerned, subject to the basic negotiating principle that nothing is definitely agreed until the whole has been agreed. Significant progress was recorded on another four to six chapters.

As such there are few major obstacles to their membership, envisaged by the Copenhagen Council for 1 January 1995. However, the negotiations will have to gather momentum in order to enlarge the EU by the 1 January 1995 target date, a date that many policymakers consider ambitious. All negotiating obstacles will have to be overcome by March 1994 at the latest, to allow for transforming the agreements into draft legal texts to be included in future Acts of Accession, translation of the eventual Accession Treaties, approval by the European Parliament, signature and national ratification procedures and referenda. Each applicant country requires a majority in a referendum to ratify accession. Perhaps the greatest obstacle to joining the EU is that most voters in three of the four candidate countries are now against membership.

2   The Finnish Application

The motivations of the Finnish government in applying to join the EU are similar to those of the other applicants. However, Finland's desire to join the EU is stronger than the other two Nordic applicants, a fact that is largely attributable to the unstable situation in the neighbouring Russian Federation and the collapse of Finland's trade with the FSU. The fall in bilateral trade with the FSU, from around a quarter of total exports in the late 1980s to only 7 per cent in 1993, contributed to the worst recession since Finnish independence, including a ten per cent fall in GDP since 1991 and a rise in unemployment to 19 per cent in May 1993. With instability and an uncertain economic environment in the East, Finland had no alternative but to apply to join the EU.

Finland is aware that EEA membership is only a step towards the ultimate goal of joining the EU. In particular, membership of the EEA does not give Finland a clear voice in EU decision-making. By becoming a full member of the EU, Finland can participate in decisions affecting its future and security.

According to the Finnish Government Institute for Economic Research, EU membership would increase real income by eight per cent, increase employment by 100,000, reduce consumer prices by 20 per cent, and provide a more stable macro-economic environment. Membership will strengthen Finnish access to the EU market, which already account for 60 per cent of Finland's trade. Membership will allow Finnish industry to compete on an equal footing with EU firms in an affluent single market of 350 million people, thereby providing opportunities for full scale economic integration, efficiency improvements and further investment. EU membership will also allow Finnish industry to participate in EU support programmes for Eastern and Central Europe and improve trading links with developing countries.

The Case Against

A common view about EU integration in Finland is that the process is somehow irresistible, even pre-ordained, because internationalisation inevitably will break down the old nation-states. Although there appears to be no other option available except to join the EU, the practical fact is that Finland does have a choice between 'artificial' and 'natural' economic integration.

'Artificial' integration refers to the formal adaptation and subordination of an economy to a dominant centre. A single productive system is formed with common rules, common money and common policies, and the smaller economy looses its autonomy. The larger core economy may or may not retain its autonomy, but its influence on the union is overwhelming. 'Natural' integration refers to a more sustainable and gradual linking up of two or several economies, which have geographical and cultural affinities. The economies formally retain much of their autonomy, even though they try to harmonise laws and standards, and co-ordinate their policies whenever possible.

The integration of Finland, Norway and Sweden into the EU would be a clear case of 'artificial' integration. A deepening of the traditional Nordic co-operation is an example of natural integration. Nordic countries are integrated to an extent which is hard to find elsewhere in the world. They have never politically, and not even culturally, belonged to the EU. They form a geographic unity, with long distances and a harsh climate. They have a long history of mutual peace, and they share the same legal traditions, culture, and religion. Scandinavian languages are spoken by 20 out of 23 million people. They all have a vibrant consensual democracy and social corporatism, a long-standing tradition of public openness, of high electoral participation and strong peoples' movements. Scandinavia also forms an economic community with a common labour market and a quarter of all trade is intra-Nordic.

The break-up of the FSU further improves the conditions for 'natural' integration. Estonia and Carelia are geographically and linguistically related to Finland. Estonia, which feels closer economically and culturally to Scandinavia than to Latvia and Lithuania, has close links with Finland and Sweden, and could become a member of the Nordic block. If Finland and Sweden were to become full members of the EU, and Estonia remained outside, it would be difficult to proceed with natural integration because their external trading relations would be determined in Brussels.

The Nordic countries have developed a unique community of their own based on common values and traditions such as: the relatively strong position of women, an universal welfare state, subsidised public services, regional equality, full employment and environmental sensitivity. Of course, many in the EU also aspire to these values, and occasionally legislation and practice is better in one EU country than in one of the Nordic countries, but it is more likely that Scandinavian values in the EU would be submerged under the different traditions of continental Europe rather than the other way around.

Scandinavian Social Democrats, who strongly favour EU membership, believe that the EU can imitate Nordic models on a larger scale. They believe in a Europe with a 'social dimension' as outlined by Commission President Delors. In reality, the Single Market and EMU look set to increase the gap between rich and poor regions; weaken coherent national productive systems; challenge social corporatism; erode the tax base; force governments to give up full employment as a central policy goal, and cause the welfare state to crumble. Furthermore, if Finland joined the EU, Finland's large number of unemployed, many of whom are young and unskilled, would compete with Southern Europeans, and possibly Eastern Europeans, who would be allowed to immigrate freely into Finland, potentially creating social conflict.

The Finnish establishment has accepted EMU and the convergence criteria of the Maastricht Treaty uncritically. Finland's in-built devaluation cycles of the post-war era were mild in relation to the boom and bust connected with the 'strong Markka' policies of the early 1990s. Joining the EMU would not prevent the wide inflationary and exchange rate fluctuations that Finland has recently experienced.

The considerable support for such arguments is reflected in opinion polls, referenda and the actions of governments in the Nordic countries. Gallup opinion polls in late November 1993 found majorities in all three Nordic applicants against membership for the first time: 41 per cent of Finns opposed membership compared to 36 per cent in favour; 48 per cent of Swedes oppose membership compared to 30 per cent in favour, and 52 per cent of Norwegians oppose membership while only 22 per cent support it. The Aland

Islands will probably conclude that their local self-government is not compatible with full EU membership. No political party in Iceland wants to apply for EU membership. Already, the Faeroe Islands and Greenland have opted to leave the EU.

3 Obstacles To Membership

The main obstacles in the accession negotiations are institutional, agricultural, regional, and environmental and health issues.

Reform of Institutions

The European Parliament and some larger Member States have stated that reforms of EU institutions are needed before any final decision can be taken on enlargement. Although MEPs voted in mid-November 1993 that institutional changes should accompany enlargement, the European Parliament is actually reluctant to hold candidates to ransom over institutional reform.

Candidates believe that reducing the size of the Commission, changing voting rules in the Council of Ministers and changing the system of selecting the presidency cannot be part of the enlargement negotiations. The electorates of candidate states must have the chance to decide to join the EU on the basis of present and known rules. Attempts to change what has been agreed would not be accepted by candidate governments and the electorates in national referenda.

Finland hopes that it and other new members will be accorded equality with member states of comparable size in EU institutions. Finland welcomes the decisions of the Copenhagen Council which provides for an early enlargement without major institutional reforms. Welcome assurances have also come from Chancellor Kohl who told the Swedish Prime Minister that there would be no attempts to reduce the influence of smaller EU nations. The Prime Minister of Belgium, Mr. Claes, has said that talks on reforming the decision-making structure should not be linked with the enlargement negotiations. Candidates believe that the 1996 Inter-

6

governmental Conference (IGC) is the proper time and place for a thorough examination of institutional questions.

Neutrality

Initially, neutrality was the major obstacle to EU membership for Austria, Finland and Sweden. However, as neutrality has lost its salience in the post-Cold War era, it is no longer regarded as an obstacle to membership.

As candidates must accept the Maastricht Treaty *in toto*, they are required to adhere to the Common Foreign and Security Policy (CFSP). As a member of the North Atlantic Treaty Organisation (NATO), the CFSP would present no problem for Norway. Perhaps suprisingly, the three neutral applicants do not believe that their particular brand of neutrality is at variance with the CFSP. For example, Finland is fully prepared to participate actively in the shaping and implementation of the CFSP because it sees no contradiction between strengthening security in Northern Europe, and the continent as a whole, and eventual Finnish membership in the EU. Finland is open to the various security options being proposed, including possible membership in the Western European Union (WEU). If Finland joins the EU, Finland will take the appropriate decisions in the light of the development of European security structures, most likely at the 1996 IGC.

Any new EU member state, whether traditionally neutral or not, which joins the WEU will, in theory, be entitled to apply to join NATO. However, the three neutral applicants, unlike Central European countries, have not publicly expressed interest in NATO membership. For example, the Foreign Minister of Finland, Mr. Haavisto, has stated that NATO membership is premature because there is no security threat that might compel Finland to make a decision to join now. Nevertheless, an enlargement of the EU could accelerate the enlargement of NATO.

The Russian Federation does not regard an enlargement of NATO in the Nordic area as threatening, but an enlargement of NATO to Central Europe would be regarded as a hostile act. In August 1993,

President Yeltsin affirmed in Warsaw the right of sovereign nations to choose their own means of ensuring their security. Since then he modified this position by saying that Russia and NATO should jointly guarantee Eastern Europe's security. The Russian Federation believes that there should be no eastwards enlargement of NATO because it would contravene the September 1990 Agreement on German reunification which prohibits the deployment of foreign troops and nuclear arms East of the Elbe.

After frequent changes in policy positions, NATO's 16 members agreed at the January 1994 summit to stop short of offering full NATO membership to East and Central Europe: no timetable was established and no concrete security guarantees were given. Although the compromise 'Partnership For Peace' formula is regarded as a second best option by Central Europe, it strikes a balance between not isolating the Russian Federation and enhancing security links with Central and East European states.

The Russian Federation believes the best solution lies in the development of a dialogue between NATO and non-NATO countries on ways of forming a joint system of pan-European security. The North Atlantic Co-operation Council (NACC) should be enlarged to cover CSCE countries and it should be transformed from an advisory into a decision-making body. Although many parts of Europe are involved in civil war, the Conference on Security and Co-operation in Europe (CSCE) continues to try to improve its capabilities in preventing conflicts and managing crises.

Agriculture

Agriculture is the most sensitive issue in the negotiations. Three of the four candidates have higher average price levels and protection for their agricultural products than the EU. The four hope/expect to maintain the same standard of living for their farmers because they believe that this expectation falls within the stated objectives of the EU's Common Agriculture Policy (CAP). In particular, Nordic countries are looking for special arrangements to accommodate Arctic agriculture.

Transitional arrangements are needed for those agricultural products where the difference between prices in the applicant countries and CAP levels and Customs Union Strategy require consideration to be given to questions of alignment and compensation after accession. Ensuring conformity with the GATT and avoiding the reinstallation of border controls in the internal market are central issues arrangements.

The Commission stated in late November 1993 that it wanted to end price support for farmers from the day of accession when local prices would be allowed to compensate farmers for the loss of state subsidies for a negotiated period. Both Austrian officials and Finnish politicians have strongly criticised the plan to cut agricultural subsidies because they believe it could undermine support for joining the EU. The negative reaction from Austria was unexpected because the EU believed that Austria's Alpine farmers would cause fewer difficulties in negotiations than their Nordic counterparts.

The announcement of the subsidy cuts is believed to have contributed to the first majority in recent Finnish opinion polls against joining the EU. Farming only employs eight per cent of the Finnish population and constitutes only 4.5 per cent of the GDP. However, it is regarded as part of the national heritage, especially given that as recently as 1960 about a third of the workforce was still employed on the land. If the Centre Party, which traditionally draws its support from rural areas, cannot achieve a suitable agreement on agriculture, the governing coalition may be in crisis. Finland wants recognition in the accession agreement that its growing season is short, and that its farms are small and distant from markets. It is also feared that Finland's security could be threatened because its 1,300 kilometre border with Russia would become depopulated if people can no longer earn a living from farming.

Regional Policy and State Aids

As future net contributors to the EU budget, the applicants are trying to maximise receipts of structural funds as a means of clawing back contributions. To prevent Arctic and mountain regions from becoming more sparsely populated than they are today, state subsidies are high and special policies have been adopted to promote economic activity. The candidate governments want to achieve an appropriate balance of EU structural measures and continuation of national subsidies.

In late November 1993, the Commission offered each of the four applicants the highest level of structural aid, Objective 1 status, for remote and poorer regions (those having an average per capita income below 75 per cent of the EU average). Objective 1 status is being offered to: Finland's three eastern provinces and Lapland; the four northern counties of Norway, and Sweden's northern-most province, Norrbotten. Although these regions are above the Objective 1 threshold, the aids have been awarded because the four will be net contributors to the EU budget and because the structural budget is unlikely to be fully disbursed. Similarly rules for state aids in remote regions are also likely to be applied flexibly to take account of huge distances and the desire to keep inaccessible border areas populated.

Environment, Health and Safety

The EU wants to ensure coherence in the internal market but the applicants are equally insistent on maintaining what they see as their own higher health, safety and environmental standards. Most of the problems are well known from the EEA Agreement where open-ended transitional periods with review clauses have been granted. Applicants have declared themselves unwilling to allow 'substandard' products into their countries.

The need to keep the free circulation of goods in the internal market and the will of the applicants to maintain more stringent health and safety standards than those of the *acquis communautaire* must be considered jointly. The EU Commission is using a three pronged-approach: it is refusing to change its position on issues, such as car emission standards, where standards are equivalent; it is offering transitional exemptions where the EU will raise standards in the future, for example on safety belts; and it will deal with the most difficult issues, such as health labelling, by granting transitional exemptions with a review, in which applicants will have a full voice, after three years.

Other Main Problem Areas

The existing state monopolies' restrictions on the production, import, export, whole-sale and retailing of alcoholic beverages, tobacco and some other products are strongly defended by many in applicant countries. Some of the applicants declare that their monopolies are based on important health and social policy considerations and that anti-drink groups will oppose any increased access to alcohol. However, adaptation of these monopolies are being examined in the light of existing EU legislation and the EU rules which candidates have already accepted for the purposes of the EEA Agreement. In the negotiations, Sweden has been allowed to keep its state monopoly on the sale of alcohol and be exempted from the EU ban on the sale of 'snus', a popular orally-taken wet snuff.

The four want to keep some restrictions on the right of residence. The applicants refer to the Danish protocol to the Maastricht Treaty restricting the purchase of secondary residences by foreigners as a precedent for maintaining such a regime after membership, even if the Edinburgh Council of December 1992 clearly stated that special arrangements for Denmark would apply exclusively to Denmark and not to other existing or acceding Member States.

As members of EFTA, all applicant countries already enjoy free trade with the EU, but as members they will be obliged to adopt the EU's common external tariff levels. Some of the four desire to maintain temporarily rates that are either higher or lower than EU rates.

All Nordic candidates want to maintain their free trade arrangements with Estonia, Latvia and Lithuania, in the expectation of a future EU-Baltic States free trade agreement and closer links with the St. Petersburg area. However, the EU is concerned that Baltic States' customs arrangements may be inadequately controlled.

The four candidates have also expressed concern about changing special arrangements with third countries, such as car imports from Japan and export quotas for agricultural exports to the United States. Budgetary matters are becoming more an issue as the nature of the transitional arrangements is becoming clearer.

There are several other issues in the negotiations which are either of interest to just one, or a few, of the applicant countries, including: the Road Transit Agreement demanded by Austria to restrict transit traffic; special arrangements for fisheries; Finnish requests that peat is regarded as a source of energy; EURATOM controls and supply contracts; specific requests concerning conservation of flora and fauna and/or hunting; and Norway's rejection of an EU directive proposing to increase competition in the energy sector, and the demand that its state oil company, Statoil, no longer have an automatic right to 50 per cent participation in exploration fields.

4 Economic and Monetary Union

The first possible date for EMU is 1997 and an automatic start is scheduled for January 1999. Both dates appear hard to achieve today because few countries will be able to fulfil the prescribed convergence criteria by then. Nevertheless, it is too early to declare EMU dead. Discussions about reform of the EMS have started, but as fundamental and meaningful reform is unlikely, there is hardly any alternative to a gradual transition from a fixed exchange rate system to a single currency.

EMU is not an obstacle to membership for the four applicant countries. Unlike the United Kingdom and Denmark, the four applicants states will not be given the opportunity to opt out of EMU. All four tried to maintain or establish fixed exchange rates in recent years unilaterally in order to prepare for future membership in the EMS. The most successful EU candidate has been Austria which has established a fixed parity with the D-Mark with very minor fluctuations. Austria has benefited from interest rates which have always been only slightly above, and sometimes even below, German rates.

The Norwegian Krone was stable in relation to a currency basket between 1986 and 1992. In 1990, it was linked, with minimal fluctuations, to the ECU with a central rate of about eight krone to the ECU. However, in December 1992, the Norwegian currency was the last Nordic country to fall victim to the European currency crisis. However, its devaluation has been comparatively small.

Sweden and Finland both tied their currencies to the ECU in 1991 with fluctuation margins of plus/minus 1.5 per cent and 3 per cent respectively. Sweden lost its fight to retain the fixed ECU rate, even though the Swedish authorities underlined their firm commitment with dramatic interest rate increases. This policy made the domestic economy hostage to volatile transactions on the foreign exchange market. High short-term interest rates were certainly not helpful in diminishing the apparent strains in the financial system and in overcoming recessionary tendencies. Therefore the market bet against the long-term sustainability of this policy, and the Swedish Krona has been floating at a lower rate since November 1992.

Faced with a 10 per cent decline in Finnish GDP in 1991 and 1992, markets were unconvinced that the chosen Markka/ECU exchange rate was realistic. The weakness in the US Dollar, tensions in the EMS before the 1992 French referendum on the Maastricht Treaty forced the Finnish government to abandon the fixed ECU rate and devalue the Markka by 12 per cent in November 1991.

The entry of the four applicant countries would not pose any major problems for EMU. They would actually enhance the goal of EMU because: they have per capita incomes above the EU average; they would be net contributors to the EU budget, and because EMU would gain four more stability-minded countries.

The four applicants stand a better chance of meeting the convergence criteria than most current EU members, in particular those from Southern Europe. According to 1992 data and the forecast for 1993, Austria meets two of the Maastricht criteria. It misses the two most important targets on inflation and on current budget deficits, but in both cases the deviation is comparatively small. Norway is also very close to meeting all four convergence criteria. However, its current budget deficit slightly exceeds the three per cent ceiling.

Finland meets the convergence criteria for inflation, long-term interest rate and outstanding debt. But the annual budget deficit of ten per cent of GDP is clearly above the ceiling. Even though there is much time left to correct the existing gap, it will not be easy to reduce the budget deficit to the required three per cent ratio. Moreover, the ratio of outstanding debt to GDP is likely to rise above the 60 per cent ceiling.

Sweden meets only the long-term interest rate criterion. The most severe problem is the 7.8 per cent of GDP current budget deficit, which in 1992 is almost four per cent above the permitted ceiling. The deficit, forecast to be over 13 per cent in 1993, would require a strict austerity policy including further heavy cuts in the Swedish welfare state to bring it below the EMU ceiling. Even with the ongoing determined government reductions and an economic recovery, it is doubtful whether Sweden can fulfil the criteria in the next few years. It will also have problems meeting the 60 per cent of outstanding debt to GDP ceiling as debt rises sharply.

Austria and Norway would have no major difficulties in meeting the EMU entry criteria in due course. However, it is doubtful that fiscal problems in Finland and Sweden can be overcome in the next few years; both countries would need strict adjustment policies to pass the EMU convergence test. The Finnish and Swedish governments will have to decide whether they want to retard expected recoveries in order to meet EMU convergence criteria, or postpone EMU membership.

The larger EMU becomes, the more difficult it will be in principle to handle. A systematic problem is that investment and economic activity will be concentrated at the centre where infrastructure is best and demand and purchasing power are above average. This means that peripheral regions may fall behind the centre in terms of growth, employment and income. An EU monetary policy cannot be regionalised and the European Central Bank would have to resist such pressure. Neutralising these centralising tendencies will require an increase in EU structural funds.

Another central question for the viability of EMU is whether it is possible to combine a centralised monetary policy with decentralised fiscal and wage policies. Without monetary and exchange rate policy-making, and with limits on fiscal policy, member states will have to implement unusual flexibility in wage policies and require large flexibility on the supply side of the economy. The problem is aggravated when external shocks occur. For example, when Finland's trade with the FSU collapsed and the Markka was tied to the D-Mark, the Finnish government had to freeze wages in order to reverse the recession.

5 Winning Referenda: Lessons From Denmark

After the accession agreements are finalised with the Commission, the candidate governments must gain the endorsement of their publics in national referenda. The negotiated agreements must be adequate enough to appeal to national publics, and governments have to sell the agreements effectively to them.

Lessons can be learned from Denmark's experience in ratifying the Maastricht Treaty. As the only member of both the Nordic Council and the EU, Denmark is regarded as the 'test laboratory' for the other Nordic countries. Although a sizeable majority in Danish Parliament recommended the Maastricht Treaty, 50.7 per cent of Danes voted against it in the first Danish referendum in June 1992. To ensure ratification of the Maastricht Treaty, the Edinburgh Council exempted Denmark from the third phase of EMU, EU defence arrangements, Euro-citizenship and police co-operation. These exemptions as well as the elaboration of the principle of subsidiarity and more transparency in the work of EU institutions enabled 56.7 per cent of Danes to vote for the treaty in the second referendum in May 1993.

The majority and high voter turnout suggested that most Danes realised it was now or never to join the European mainstream. The exemptions do not mean that Denmark has said no forever to a single currency or to a common defence. However, as agreed by seven of the eight Danish parties supporting the Edinburgh compromise, if Denmark changes its mind in the future, another referendum will be required on these issues.

The two referenda in Denmark and the one in France on the Maastricht Treaty indicate that complex EU issues should never again be perceived as solely the business of an elite of bureaucrats, lobbyists, and a small group of politicians. Political debate on European issues must be accompanied by a parallel public debate. Politicians must inform the voters properly, and they must try to influence public opinion with strong and easily understood arguments that make people think. Attempts must also be made to coordinate the views of important interest groups. If EU issues cannot be widely understood, then it is the fault of politicians and opinion formers, and not the public.

Denmark is taking some new initiatives to ensure that members of parliament and the Danish population will be more involved in EU debates by changing the EU decision-making process. A council with 150 members is being established with representatives of grassroots movements, and members of the Folketing's market committee and the European Parliament. This council will be a forum for debate and it will advise parliament and the government concerning general problems and issues. Various parliamentary committees will be involved much more directly than before with EU issues, gradually widening the circle of politicians familiar with EU issues beyond the current 17 members of the market committee. In addition, an EU public information office has been opened in the Folketing to better inform politicians.

In the case of future referenda on membership in the Nordic countries, the timing could be important in building momentum for enlargement. The first referendum might be held in the country whose public is most in favour of joining followed by the next most likely country to vote in favour. A Yes vote in Finland, where the first referendum is likely to held in September 1994, could be important in building support for membership in Sweden and Norway. If the Finns and the Swedes vote in favour of membership, the Norwegians, the most sceptical of the three, may fear isolation, and vote to join the EU.

6 Eastern Neighbouring States

The Russian Federation, Central Europe and the Baltic States are too important, politically and economically, to be ignored. With the end of the Cold War, it is possible to expand the EU not only to Northern Europe but also to Central and Eastern Europe. Should the EU not enlarge eastwards, the failure could destabilise nascent eastern democracies.

The Edinburgh Council proposals for EU enlargement form the basis for further integration of Central European and Baltic States. Although future association and the necessary conditions for signing Europe Agreements were decided at the Copenhagen summit, no timetable was established. After Malta and Cyprus, the Visegrad countries (the Czech Republic, Hungary, Poland and Slovakia) are the next most likely members, possibly joining around the year 2000. Next on the waiting list are the Baltic states, Bulgaria and Romania which constitute an ill-defined group. Membership of the Russian Federation and Albania are much longer-term possibilities.

Potential candidates from Central and Eastern Europe must be patient. It took years for Spain and Portugal to be even considered for EU membership. Thereafter, it took eight years from the beginning of negotiations to the entering into force of the accession treaty. Transitional arrangements took another seven years to complete.

The Russian Federation
Democratic changes in Russia remove the political, military and economic basis for its isolation in Europe. Russia no longer views

European integration negatively and it is ready for rapprochement and co-operation with the EU. It respects the right of every sovereign state to join the EU, and understands the reasons which motivate countries to join.

Russia wants a contractual and legal base for a long-term relationship with the EU. The late 1993 agreement with the EU was not as substantive and thoroughly balanced as Russia wanted. It is in Europe's interest to have a common European economic space based on the principles of free trade and non-discrimination. A new Europe separated by a 'Gold Curtain' should not replace the old Europe separated by the Iron Curtain. Russia is willing to live by GATT and IMF rules and it wants free trade with the EU. Although the EU and the G7 support Russia's market reforms, the EU still discriminates against trade with Russia on the grounds that it still has mainly a state trading structure. Trade should at least be conducted on a Most Favoured Nation basis. However, many in the West believe that Russia must make more progress with its market reforms before it gains improved access to Western markets.

The Visegrad Countries

Many Central Europeans believe that they would be members of the EU today had the Yalta Agreement in 1945 not resulted in the retardation of their economic development. Their wish to join the EU is therefore an attempt to catch up with history. However, as EU membership is unlikely in the short-term, Poland and the other three Visegrad countries hope that trade links will be increased, the scope of political dialogue will be broadened, involvement in the mechanisms of European political co-operation will be increased, and that foreign assistance will be adapted to meet the current requirements of the transformation process including, in particular, infrastructure development.

The Europe Agreements, negotiated first with the former Czechoslovakia, Hungary and Poland, and subsequently with Bulgaria and Romania, are a reflection of the political determination to include the region in the EU's integration process. However, as of September 1993, they have been ratified by only seven of the 12 EU countries. Only the trade section, the so-called Interim Agreement, is binding. The Visegrad countries therefore hope that the process will be completed as soon as possible so that the Agreement can enter into force in 1994.

The essential weakness of Poland's Europe Agreement lies in the fact that it concentrates on defining the principles of trade and economic co-operation. It liberalises economic relations with the EU in an extremely limited and selective way. For example, it introduces extensive trade liberalisation in industrial goods, but very little in agricultural trade. EU measures continue to protect 'sensitive' areas in which Poland is increasing exports. These measures have an enormous impact on the volume of Polish exports but constitute only a fraction of the EU's total market. The Agreement by-passes the question of giving EU companies structural funds and periods in which to adjust gradually to Eastern competition. Similarly, significant liberalisation is adopted with regard to the establishment of undertakings, which is of great significance to the free movement of capital, but the free movement of persons is still strictly limited.

Poland's Europe Agreement is weighted in Poland's favour solely in structural terms. Many of the provisions which were intended to assist Poland as the weaker partner have no more than potential significance. For example, certain quotas and tariff ceilings granted to Poland cannot be enjoyed since it does not produce some of the products covered by the concessions. EU trade concessions are also often linked to numerous trade and other instruments, such as fixing a high minimum price for soft fruit, which partially negate the effect of concessions. Such protectionist measures may not be inconsistent with the letter of Europe Agreement, but they are inconsistent with its spirit.

Some Western businessmen believe these protective mechanisms are justified because Eastern countries do not have *inter alia* bankruptcy and competition laws, and proper pricing mechanisms for inputs, particularly labour. Furthermore, it is not politically easy to open domestic markets when foreign competition is regarded as unfair and when national and EU structural funds are inadequate.

As they have unfavourable trade balances with the EU, the Visegrad countries believe they are making a greater contribution to the creation of jobs in the EU than a reduction of them. For example, the Polish trade deficit alone accounts for 200,000 jobs in the EU. If the EU continues to deny market access to Eastern goods, it may be necessary for Central and East European countries to introduce either direct or indirect import restrictions, such as lowering the exchange rate, which would damage EU exports and employment in the EU.

On the political level, the Europe Agreement establishes some form of political dialogue. However, the EU felt unable to issue an unequivocal declaration on future membership. Not only must a date be set for starting enlargement negotiations, but political dialogue should take on increasingly advanced forms leading to participation, even in an observer capacity, in EU bodies which take decisions affecting co-operation.

Poland's long-term aim is to join the EU. Poland's gradual social, economic and political transformation is taking it closer to a position when it will be eligible to join. The Copenhagen document of the 1993 European Council already lists all the conditions relating to the assumption of obligations to join the EU. There is no need to supplement those obligations with additional criteria, particularly quantitative criteria. Fixing new criteria to supplement the general conditions and objectives for enlargement did not occur when Greece, Portugal and Spain joined.

Poland is willing to assume all the provisions of the Treaties of Rome and Maastricht. The remaining factors and requirements, including the timetable for change, the length of the transitional period, and the speed at which specific obligations are entered into, can be agreed once negotiations have been initiated. As the date for EU Membership has yet to be fixed, the Polish government believes formal negotiations should begin no later than immediately after the 1996 IGC.

The French proposal submitted to the Luxembourg Council contains criteria which could potentially delaying further enlargement. In particular, the level of per capita GDP is incompatible with the Visegrad Memorandum drafted at the Edinburgh Summit which stated that evaluation of candidate's economies should be based on their health rather than level of income. The budgetary consequences of the eventual accession of the Visegrad countries are also exaggerated.

The Copenhagen Council's document "Towards a closer association with the countries of Central and Eastern Europe" amends certain provisions contained in the Europe Agreement, a positive development, especially given that it was drafted against a background of deepening recession in most EU countries. The document looks upon future membership of associate countries favourably. It recommends that PHARE funds be released for infrastructure projects and that Polish goods be allowed improved access to the EU market, in particular 'sensitive' goods, although the overall direct benefits are relatively small, an additional ECU 100 million in exports over five years. However, the references to political dialogue are inadequate, especially as regards direct participation in EU bodies which affect the interests of the Visegrad group.

The Baltic States

Estonian President Lenart Meri has stated that his country "belongs to a region where Central Europe imperceptibly changes into Northern Europe". As sovereign democratic European states, the three Baltic States are formally entitled to become EU members. That the accession of the three Baltic States would result in an EU of over 20 members is not an argument against enlarging the EU because it is the EU's own responsibility to make itself fit for enlargement.

The Baltic states, particularly Estonia and Latvia, have undertaken sweeping democratic reforms since independence in 1991, including the introduction of multiparty systems; a free and independent media; price, foreign investment and fiscal reforms; the creation of independent currencies; the abolition of state trading and privatisation of state enterprises.

The collapse in Baltic States' trade with the republics of the FSU, largely due to economic decline, customs restrictions, poor bank clearing systems, and the ending of state trading, have led to a reorientation of trade towards EFTA and the EU. For example, Since 1990, Estonian trade with the FSU collapsed from 95 per cent of trade to only 15 per cent in 1993. In the same period, trade with EFTA states has grown from two to 36 per cent, and trade with the EU has increased from one per cent of trade to 20 per cent. Nevertheless, Estonia continues to promote transit trade with Russia through its ports, and it expects that substantial trade with Russia will resume once the economic situation in Russia has stabilised.

Closer economic links, and the likelihood that major trading partners like Finland and Sweden will join the EU, is propelling the Baltic States to form closer links with the EU. The success of the EFTA free trade model inspired the September 1993 Baltic Free Trade Agreement. By signing this agreement, the Baltic states have signalled their readiness to negotiate a free trade agreement with the EU, and ultimately their ability to integrate into the EU. Although the Baltic States prime ministers have issued a common statement reiterating their commitment to moving towards full integration into EU structures, by accepting the *acquis communautaire*, the Baltic States' current approaches to association with the EU differ.

Estonia aims to transform the current asymmetric situation in which it unilaterally offers an open market to the outside world into a fully symmetrical relationship along the lines of the EU-EFTA free trade model. It has implemented a trade and co-operation accord with the EU providing for MFN status, and a mandate has been given to the Commission to develop this accord into a free trade agreement. Estonia has indicated its preference for an association or Europe Agreement. However, considering Estonia's liberal trade policies, rapid transformation towards a free market and the difficulties in implementing the association agreements at the moment, Estonia believes full integration into the EU would be more effective.

Latvia's trade and economic co-operation agreeement with the EU makes it eligible for trade preferences under the EU's Generalised System of Preferences (GSP). GSP status allows Latvian exporters to have market access on a level playing field with its major competitors. However, the high level of subsidised agriculture in the EU, makes it difficult for Latvia to obtain significant concessions in agricultural trade. Given the speed with which Latvia has re-established a market economy and democracy, it hopes that it will accede to the EU before the year 2000.

Lithuania regards future free trade agreements between the EU and Baltic States as interim agreements which later could be developed into Europe Agreements. An Europe Agreement is both the Lithuanian government's short-term and optimal framework for developing the association with the EU because it embraces a wide range of areas for co-operation and leaves enough room for specific approaches.

In sum, it is in the best interest of the Baltic States, that the EU:

1. eliminates restrictions in existing trading arrangements;

2. guarantees that enlargement will not impair existing free trade arrangements with Scandinavian countries;

3. concludes treaties of association with the Baltic states, explicitly providing for eventual membership as envisaged by the Copenhagen Summit;

4. strengthens the political dialogue and announces that it will launch negotiations on full membership with the Baltic States at the same time as with Central European countries;

5. pledges its full support for the Baltic states' efforts to establish good neighbourly relations with the Russian Federation.

Relations Between the Russian Federation and the Baltic States

The withdrawal of Russian troops and the rights of the Russian-speaking minority in each Baltic state will be the key determinants in the relationship between the Russian Federation and the Baltic States.

The Russian Federation appears to be linking the withdrawal of its troops to an improvement in the rights of Russian-speaking minorities. Russia believes that the withdrawal of its troops is a transitional issue in establishing normal relations. Although Russia has reached a compromise with Lithuania, the withdrawal of troops from Latvia and Estonia must be regulated by appropriate agreements and social guarantees for service men and their families.

The treatment of the Russian-speaking minority in Estonia raises the greatest concern not only in Russia, but also in Finland and elsewhere. Estonian legislation on aliens, citizenship, language, local elections, and education are perceived to discriminate against the Russian-speaking minority. Recent decisions of the Tallinn and Tartu City Councils to force Russian servicemen and military pensioners out of their apartments are an example of this. Although some concrete steps have been made by Estonian leaders to relax inter-ethnic tensions, such as minor amendments to the Aliens Law, there has not been a dramatic change in the treatment of ethnic Russians.

The Estonian Government believes that criticism of their laws are unfounded. Russians in Estonia enjoy a higher standard of living and more liberties than they would do in Russia. The Estonian government believes the Russian minority should integrate, especially given that Estonian citizenship may be gained by demonstrating a basic proficiency in Estonian of only 1,500 words.

When a new government came to power in Latvia, Russia noted a decline in anti-Russian rhetoric and a growing interest in political dialogue. President Ulmanis' intention to convene a National Forum with the participation of a representative of the national minorities to discuss the Citizenship Law was a positive step. Russia hopes that the Latvian authorities will engage in bilateral discussions and realise the danger of adopting the previous government's proposal to expel the Russian population. In light of Latvia's willingness to become a member of the Council of Europe, approbation of the draft Citizenship Law by Council of Europe and CSCE experts is another sign that the situation is improving.

7 Conclusions

1. For some EU member states the attraction of widening is to slow the deepening tendancies of more federalist EU countries by recruiting other minimalist partners to join the EU. Even though the Maastricht Treaty checks the centralising tendencies of the EU, a widened EU will inevitably require a deepening of the integration process.

2. With the end of the Cold War, EU enlargement must not create new lines of division in Europe. Europe cannot afford to have two sides of the same continent moving in opposite directions: one becoming richer and more closely integrated while the other becomes poorer and disintegrates.

3. The four applicants can exert a positive influence on the EU, making it less protectionist, being net contributors to the budget, and pushing the EU closer towards the goal of EMU. The four candidates are likely to meet the EMU convergence criteria sooner and more easily than most existing EU member states.

4. Given the virtual collapse of its trade with the FSU and the end of the Cold War, EU membership is Finland's only alternative. Public opinion in Finland about EU membership is more favourable than that in Sweden and Norway because Finland looks upon EU membership as an insurance policy against political and economic instability in the neighbouring Russian Federation.

5. Although good progress has been made on all subjects in the enlargement negotiations, it will require exceptional efforts from all parties to meet the 1 January 1995 target date for membership. Although the accepted deadline for completing negotiations is March 1994, some in applicant states believe that the real deadline for achieving membership is before the 1996 IGC.

6. In late 1993, the negotiations entered the most sensitive phase as the most difficult issues (agriculture, regional aid and EU decision-making) were discussed. Candidate governments

want fair treatment on these and other issues, otherwise they fear that they will be unable to sell the accession agreements to their publics, and gain a majority in national referenda on EU accession. It is essential that politicians communicate the complex issues surrounding membership clearly to voters.

7. EFTA candidate countries are desired by the EU but the populations in most EFTA candidates are not sure that they want to join. By contrast, Central European states are not as much desired by the EU, yet both their governments and citizens are eager to join.

8. The sooner the current accession process is completed, the sooner the EU can begin to focus on problems in Central and Eastern Europe. It is vital for both the EU and candidate states to have stable neighbours.

9. As enlargement of the EU to the East is unlikely in the short-term, the Central and East European countries are concentrating on gaining improved access to EU markets. The EU must reduce protection because most commitments in the Europe Agreements with Central European countries are declaratory and relate to future potential. The trade concessions that exist relate to less important areas and exclude 'sensitive' areas where Central Europeans have comparative advantage. The EU must rise above protectionist tendencies, and take a longer-term view of European developments. The choice is to either to deepen and include Central and East Europe, or exclude and destabilise them.

10. Russia cannot be left out of the EU integration process. A Russia isolated from the EU and an enlarged NATO is a recipe for tension and instability. In particular, expanding NATO eastwards without building links with Russia would be a mistake. Russia should not be left out of new European security arrangements nor should it be discriminated against in trading relationships. As a country that is aspiring to have a market economy, MFN trading status should be extended to the Russian Federation (it is better to have a bear as a friend than to leave it hungry in the near-by forest!)

11. If the Baltic States are not extended improved economic and political links with the EU, the three states could again become marginalised. The EU should follow Nordic trade initiatives

and conclude free trade with the Baltic States. In the longer term, the EU should undertake membership negotiations with the Baltic States at the same time as Central European states.

List of Participants

AHO, Esko: Prime Minister of Finland and Chairman of the Centre Party of Finland

AIRINEN, Heljä: YES TO EUROPE Movement, Helsinki; freelance journalist

ANDERSSON, Jan Otto: Åbo Akademi University, Finland

ANTOLA, Esko: University of Turku, Finland

BARRINGTON, Anne: Department of Foreign Affairs, Dublin

BILLINGS, Bradley: Pew Economic Freedom Fellows Program and Georgetown University School of Foreign Service, Washington DC

BJÖRKLUND, Otto: Nokia Group, Helsinki

BLOMBERG, Jaakko: Ministry of Foreign Affairs, Helsinki

BOGOMAZOV, V M: Ministry of Foreign Affairs, Moscow

BOILLAT, Dominique: Swiss Radio International, Berne

BROWN, Tony: The Labour Party, Dublin

BUSSMANN, Hans-Werner: Federal Ministry of Foreign Affairs, Bonn

CARREWYN, Leopold: Counsellor; Ministry of Foreign Affairs, Brussels

CLARE, William: British Embassy, Helsinki

CLARK, Gerald: Royal College of Defence Studies, London

DEICHMANN, Philipp: Federal Ministry of Foreign Affairs, Bonn

DENTON, Geoffrey: Wilton Park, Steyning

DOMARKAS, Vladislovis: Deputy Foreign Minister, Vilnius

FABBRI, Fabio: European Commission, Brussels

FAIRLIE, Lyndelle: San Diego State University, San Diego

FAST, Leif: Finnish Committee for Wilton Park, Helsinki

FISCHER, Viggo: Member, Danish Parliament, Copenhagen

FORSMAN, Sven: Confederation of Finnish Industries and Employers, Helsinki

GLUHOV, A I: Ministry of Foreign Affairs, Moscow

GRANELL, Francisco: Commission of the European Communities, Brussels

GRÖNBERG, Tom: Ministry of Foreign Affairs, Helsinki
HAAVISTO, Heikki: Minister of Foreign Affairs, Helsinki
HAGELBERG, Anders: Ministry of Foreign Affairs, Stockholm
HAIKONEN, Jyrki: Centre for Finnish Business and Policy Studies (EVA), Helsinki
HAMILO, Esko: Ministry of Foreign Affairs, Helsinki
HEATHCOAT-AMORY, David: Minister of State, Foreign and Commonwealth Office, London
HEGG, Jan Wesse: Ministry of Foreign Affairs, Oslo
HERING, Berndt: Member, Bavarian Land Parliament, Munich
HIMANEN, Hannu: Ministry for Foreign Affairs, Helsinki
HØJBERG, Anne-Else: NATO, Brussels
HOPE, Marcus: Foreign and Commonwealth Office, London
HOPKINSON, Nicholas: Wilton Park, Steyning
HUHTANIEMI, Pekka: Prime Minister's Office, Helsinki
ILONIEMI, Jaakko: Centre for Finnish Business and Policy Studies (EVA), Helsinki
INGVANEZ, John: Ministry of Foreign Affairs, Malta
JÄGERHORN, Inger: *Dagens Nyheter*, Stockholm
KARKLINS, Janis: Latvian Embassy, Helsinki
KARLSSON, Ingmar: Ministry of Foreign Affairs, Stockholm
KIVIVEN, Olli: *Helsingin Sanomat*, Helsinki
KÖHLER, Jarl: Central Association of Finnish Forest Industries and Finnish Forest Industries Federation, Helsinki
LAAJAVA, Jaakko: Ministry for Foreign Affairs, Helsinki
LAANEMAE, Riho: Ministry of Foreign Affairs, Tallinn
LANG, Nicolas: Department of Foreign Affairs, Berne
LERNHART, Andreas: Federation of Austrian Industrialists, Vienna
LYALL-GRANT, Mark: Foreign and Commonwealth Office, London
MARTIN, Dominic: Foreign and Commonwealth Office, London
NAVARRO, Miguel: Prime Minister's Office, Madrid
NIINISTÖ, Sauli: Member, Finnish Parliament , Helsinki
NORDRUM, Per: *Aftenposten*, Oslo
NORQVIST, Margareta: Kommerskollegium, Stockholm
PAASIO, Pertti: Chairman, Parliamentary Foreign Affairs Committee; former Finnish Foreign Minister
PAVLOVSKIS, Olgerts: State Minister of Foreign Trade and EC Affairs, Riga

REIMAA, Markku: Ministry for Foreign Affairs, Helsinki
SALOLAINEN, Pertti: Deputy Prime Minister and Minister for Foreign Trade, Helsinki
SARALEHTO, Sampsa: Central Chamber of Commerce of Finland, Helsinki
SARYUSZ-WOLSKI, Jacek: Council of Ministers, Warsaw
SATULI, Antti: Ministry of Foreign Affairs, Helsinki
SAUER, Peter: Federal Ministry of Defence, Bonn
SCHOOF, Eberhard: EC Committee of the German Bundestag, Bonn
SCHRÖDER, Ulrich: Deutsche Bank Research, Frankfurt
SCHWAB, Klaus: Austrian Federal Economic Chamber, Vienna
SIPILÄ, Juha: YTV (Helsinki Metropolitan Area Council), Helsinki
SOININVAARA, Osmo: Helsinki City Board; former Member of Parliament
SPELLER, Paul: UK Permanent Representation to the European Commission, Brussels
STAUNER, Gabriele: Bavarian State Ministry for Federal and European Affairs, Munich
von STADEN, Berndt: former State Secretary, Foreign Office, Bonn
SUNDBÄCK, Veli: Ministry of Foreign Affairs, Helsinki
SZELAGOWSKA, Grazyna: Bureau of Interparliamentary Relations, SEJM, Warsaw
TALLQVIST, Charlotte: Deutsche Bank, Frankfurt
TALVITIE, Heikki: Ministry of Foreign Affairs, Helsinki
THORNE, Nicholas: British Embassy, Helsinki
TRANHOLM-MIKKELSEN, Jeppe: Ministry of Foreign Affairs, Copenhagen
VAAH TORANTA, Tapani: Foreign Policy Institute, Helsinki
VALLASTER, Kornelia: Federal Chancellery, Vienna
VAUBEL, Dietrich: Federal Ministry of the Interior, Bonn
VELLISTE, Trivimi: Minister of Foreign Affairs, Tallinn
VESIKANSA, Jyrki: Journalist, Helsinki
VETTE, Markus: Member, Brandenburg Land Parliament, Potsdam
WEIDUNG, Anders: University of Uppsala, Sweden
WILTON, Woulter: EC Delegation in Finland, Helsinki
WOKER, Daniel: Embassy of Switzerland, Paris
WÖRSDÖRFER, Mechthild: Federation of German Industry, Brussels

Printed in the United Kingdom for HMSO
Dd297740 2/94 C5 G3397 10170

30